*mexicasa

* mexicasa

The Enchanting Inns and Haciendas of Mexico

Photographs by

Melba Levick

Text by

Gina Hyams

CHRONICLE BOOKS

SAN FRANCISCO

DEDICATION

For my husband, Hugh Levick, my cherished travel companion, who shared in the great pleasure of creating this book.

M.L.

···

For my five-year-old daughter, Annalena, because she loves room service.

G.H.

···

Photographs copyright © 2001 by Melba Levick. Text copyright © 2001 by Gina Hyams. All rights reserved. No part of this book may be reproduced in any form without written permission from the publisher.

Library of Congress Cataloging-in-Publication Data: available.
ISBN: 0-8118-2806-9
Printed in Hong Kong

Designed by David Comberg and Vivien Sung

Distributed in Canada by
Raincoast Books
9050 Shaughnessy Street
Vancouver, British Columbia V6P 6E5

10 9 8 7 6 5 4 3 2 1

Chronicle Books LLC
85 Second Street
San Francisco, California 94105
www.chroniclebooks.com

TABLE OF CONTENTS

INTRODUCTION

"It is alarming that publications devoted to architecture have banished from their pages the words **Beauty, Inspiration, Magic, Spellbound, Enchantment,** as well as the concepts of **Serenity, Silence, Intimacy,** and **Amazement.** All these have nestled in my soul."

Mexican architect Luis Barragán (1902–1988)

The poetic qualities that Barragán so treasured thrive in the Mexican inns, haciendas, and small hotels featured in this book. Rich with history and human touch, these retreats offer a stirring antidote to sterile First World notions of good taste. Here comfort and whimsy go hand in hand—one can't help but smile at the surprise of a shocking pink *palapa* (thatched-roof dwelling) or at finding a folk art papier-mâché skeleton tucked in the back of a closet. ❋ The twenty-one destinations range from a four-hundred-year-old stone-walled convent in Oaxaca to parrot-hued contemporary villas on Mexico's Pacific Coast. Found in romantic legends, one sumptuous hotel is situated in a hacienda supposedly built by conquistador Hernán Cortés to shelter his Indian interpreter and lover, Malinche, and another, located in a Moorish Baroque mansion, was built by a smitten Spanish marquis to impress a nun. There are guest rooms in Yucatán jungle cottages where archeologists lived during the 1920s while excavating nearby ruins, and lovely B&Bs in the former homes of an eighteenth-century silver tycoon and a nineteenth-century coffee baron. Candlelit gourmet restaurants exist in factories where sisal and sugarcane were once processed, and on a cliff above the sea in Zihuatanejo, hammocks sway at a Gauguin-inspired artistic refuge created by New York bohemians. ❋ Since ancient times, the people of Mexico have demonstrated an over-the-top flair and

OPPOSITE: La Casa de la Marquesa was supposedly built by a smitten Spanish nobleman to woo a nun. *ABOVE:* This wall at Hacienda de Cortés has been crumbling for four centuries.

ABOVE: **A chair pays homage to artist Frida Kahlo at La Casa Que Canta.**
BELOW: **In Casa Luna B&B's New Room, sheer muslin floats across the wall above a feather bed topped with Guatemalan throw pillows and an embroidered, purple Spanish shawl.**

affection for unbridled color and ornamentation. To attract the attention of the gods, the Mayans and Aztecs adorned their massive temple pyramids with magnificent frescoes and intricately carved stone panels, mosaics, and statuary. Extraordinary builders, the Mayans invented the corbelled vault, which is a distinctive arch composed of projecting bricks that dispensed with the need to undergird the base of a structure. ❈ After the Conquest of 1521, the Spaniards took full advantage of the indigenous architectural talent. The crusading friars used Indian builders and craftsmen to construct hundreds of churches and monastery towns. However, the Indians adapted native building techniques and materials and infused the Gothic, Romanesque, Renaissance, and Moorish designs with a uniquely Mexican sense of color and embellishment. ❈ The Spaniards accumulated vast fortunes by exporting New World natural resources such as gold, silver, vanilla, and balsam, and by cultivating cattle. In 1565, the Philippines came under Spanish rule, and the trade routes that opened up brought Oriental influences to Mexico and enabled wealthy citizens to buy exotic silks, ivory, and hand-painted Chinese wallpaper. ❈ From the early seventeenth century through the mid-eighteenth century, *criollos* (Mexican-born Spaniards) and Indian builders embraced the Spanish Baroque style with extraordinary fervor; in their hands it became ultra-Baroque. They applied lavish, overwhelming decorative detail to both churches and private homes. In Puebla, potters began making polychromatic tin-glazed earthenware, called *Talavera* because it resembled the ceramics from the Spanish town Talavera de la Reina. During Mexico's Baroque period, gleaming Talavera tiles were used to decorate entire building facades, church domes, fountains, staircases, and kitchens. Today such tiles are seen everywhere from sinks to swimming pools. ❈ The 1821 War for Independence brought the end of Spanish rule, but the privileged class continued to take its design cues from Europe. French and Italian influences inspired palatial architecture—sweeping terraces, marble statuary, plant-filled patios, and extravagant formal gardens. Economic growth, political stability, and the veneration of European fashions characterized the long reign of President Porfirio Díaz (roughly 1876–1911). Mexican architects freely mixed and matched Gothic Revival, Renaissance, Romanesque, Victorian, Moorish, Baroque, Rococo, Neoclassical, and eventually Art Nouveau styles to suit any aristocratic whim. ❈ During the Revolution of 1910 and before the land reform that followed, many of the grand estates were ransacked or burned. The first postrevolutionary government, under Álvaro Obregón, placed great emphasis on national identity and pride, with special attention given to Indian traditions and folk art. It was the era of the great Mexican muralists: Diego Rivera, David Alfaro Siquieros, and José Clemente Orozco. ❁ The twentieth century saw the rise of modern architecture in Mexico, which was a movement led by renowned architects Luis Barragán and Ricardo Legorreta. Their minimalist, sculptural concrete buildings were painted luminous shades and continue to influence today. ❁ Mexico is a complex feast for the senses—a land bursting with spice, color, and music. It's one of the few places left on the planet where time is still time and not just money. These inns embody the Mexican spirit by enveloping guests in the soul-satisfying luxury of the *hecho a mano* (made by hand): fresh-squeezed orange juice served in hand-blown goblets, a hammered-tin mirror above a custom-glazed Talavera sink, a sinuous wrought-iron banister, a hand-loomed magenta bedspread, one-of-a-kind Zapotec rugs underfoot, a Huichol shaman's yarn painting, a barroom wall hand-stenciled to look like lace, a quirky lamp forged from an antique typewriter, patio chairs made of willow branches, a swimming pool shaped like a lagoon, and a *palapa* roof that took four acres' worth of palm fronds to thatch. The examples are endless. These places reflect the unique personalities of their visionary owners, some of whom aim to meticulously restore historic properties to their original states, and some of whom view the properties as launching pads for flights of fancy. ❁ Luis Barragán strived to create "emotional architecture"—something he described as "scenery for the theater of life." If there were equally valid solutions to a problem, he chose the one that delivered a message of beauty and drama over that which was merely efficient. The Mexican retreats celebrated in this book were all created with pleasure as the guiding design principle. The resulting spaces—vibrant, sensual, serene, and sometimes just plain goofy—are, indeed, scenery for the theater of life.

—G.H.

ABOVE: **At Casas de Careyes, a *palapa* roof soars overhead.**
BELOW: **These Talavera tiles were crafted in Dolores Hidalgo.**

❋ HACIENDA KATANCHEL

KATANCHEL'S MAYAN NAME means "Where one asks the arc of the sky." Third-century C.E. ruins found on the site suggest that ancient Mayan priests used this corner of the jungle as an observatory to track the celestial progress of the gods. Located fifteen miles east of the Yucatán's Colonial capital, Mérida, the hacienda dates back to the seventeenth century, when it was built as a cattle ranch. ❋ Hacienda Katanchel became an immensely prosperous plantation during the *henequén* (sisal) boom of the nineteenth century. The strong fiber of Mexican *Agave-sislana* cactus leaves (then known as *oro verde*, or "green gold") was exported worldwide for the manufacture of rope. This opulent era ended abruptly in the 1950s, when nylon and petroleum by-products replaced *henequén* as the core ingredient for creating rope. ❋ By the time current owners Mónica Hernández and Aníbal González discovered the property in 1996, it had been abandoned for some thirty-five years. For a while, they weren't quite sure exactly what they'd acquired, as the 740 acres were wild with dense jungle vegetation. Buildings were crumbling and hidden, and the trees had grown up through floors and walls and had even penetrated the thirty-foot-high ceilings. Gradually the tangled growth was cleared away and the grandeur of the estate was revealed. ❋ Before starting reconstruction, González, an architect originally from Seville, studied old photographs of the hacienda, consulted local archeologists about Mayan art, and researched Spanish Colonial architecture. The resulting restoration of the hacienda buildings is an inventive blend of Mexican, Spanish, and Mayan traditions. ❋ The formerly modest homes of the plantation workers were refurbished with spartan luxury into thirty-nine guest pavilions, all with private terraces, inviting hammocks, and Mayan-style gardens featuring a mix of decorative, fragrant, edible, and medicinal plants. More than eighty species of birds have been spotted on the hacienda's lush grounds. Many of the pavilions also have individual plunge pools filled with invigorating mineral water that is pumped by early-twentieth-century windmills. ❋ The Tienda de Raya, a traditional general store and wage payment center on the premises, was transformed into a library filled with hundreds of volumes about Mayan art, history, and medicinal plants. Some of the volumes are as much as a century old. The Casa de Máquinas, formerly a sisal processing factory, became an elegant restaurant serving nouvelle Yucatecan specialties such as grilled chicken in bougainvillea-petal sauce and salmon topped with *chaya*, which is a local leaf similar to spinach that is said to contain potent healing powers that cleanse the body of toxins. ❋

OPPOSITE: The stately Gran Salón, where drinks are served before and after dinner, is furnished with a mix of fine antiques from Europe, Mexico, and India, and with family heirlooms, such as Mónica Hernández's huge Persian rug (circa 1820), which hangs as a tapestry. *ABOVE:* Hacienda Katanchel's deep red exterior is painted with traditional *cal*, a mixture of natural red minerals, ground limestone, water, and *nopales* cactus juice.

ABOVE: Three graceful arches, adorned with white-cotton drapery welcome guests to Casa Principal.
RIGHT: The warm ocher-colored walls of the Casa Principal's back veranda contrast beautifully with the burnished red tile floor. The large ceramic pot on the right is a replica of a Mayan one that was used to store seeds in the 1300s.

The entrance veranda features striking original walls stenciled in pale blue, red, white, and gray geometric patterns. The seating area is composed of vintage rattan chairs and a nineteenth-century mahogany bench and table from India.

OPPOSITE: Nineteenth-century illustrations of birds by Audubon and others decorate the Casa Principal foyer. On the floor next to the silk brocade chairs is a green-tinged copper vessel from Santa Clara del Cobre.

ABOVE: The Spa Room walls are stenciled in calming shades of blue and russet. The bougainvillea petals are used in the decadent "honey body mask with flower petals," which is one of many pampering treatments available.

The Game Room has a bold geometric-tiled floor. Above the billiard table is a copper lighting fixture from San Miguel de Allende. Toward the rear is an Indonesian birdcage shaped like a Victorian house, the door of which is always left open to allow the local birds to come and go as they please.

TOP: Aníbal González designed
the stylish white cast-iron guest
beds. They are covered with fine
Portuguese linens.

MIDDLE: Situated conveniently next
to the bar, this Chinese daybed (circa
1870), upholstered with contemporary French fabric and circled by
matching chairs, is fit for a queen
holding court.

BOTTOM: Everybody adores the *burro*
Margarita, who is the hacienda's ver-
sion of the Pony Express. She stands
ready to take guests and their bag-
gage to their pavilions. She pulls a
tram along tracks left over from the
hacienda's sisal plantation days.

OPPOSITE, TOP: The restaurant and entertainment rooms are located in the Casa de Máquinas (machine house), which is the former plantation factory where *Agave-sislana* cactus leaves were processed into rope fiber.

OPPOSITE, BOTTOM: Thick black beams add sculptural drama to the restaurant, which specializes in Yucatecan regional delicacies. Mónica Hernández designed the blue glass goblets and had them handblown by craftsmen in Mexico City.

BELOW: This Colonial-era Mexican cabinet—gilded with gold leaf and hand painted—was a Mexico City flea-market find. The Talavera vases, made by masters Gorky González and Capelo of Guanajuato, are capped with decorative blue and silver glass balls from Mexico City. In Colonial times, such glass balls served a functional as well as aesthetic purpose, in that they were used to reflect and amplify candlelight.

❋ HOTEL CASA DEL BALAM

Mérida, Yucatán

THERE WEREN'T MANY tourists in the Yucatán back in the 1920s, but most of those who visited the northern port of Progreso, where the Ward Line cruise ships stopped, were met by a courtly gentleman named Fernando Barbachano Peón. He would engage the passengers in conversation right off the boat, show them a photo album of the newly excavated Mayan ruins, and invite them to stay for a week at his guest house in Mérida to see the temples for themselves. From the capital, he'd escort the visitors on the 5 A.M. two-hour train ride to Dzitas, followed by an eight-hour drive to Chichén Itzá—a ten-hour journey that today takes but an hour and a half. ❋ Casa del Balam was the Barbachano family home. Their granddaughter Isabel has re-created the house as a five-star hotel. She furnished the hotel with dark Old World antiques in the eclectic combination of Spanish, Baroque, and French styles favored by the wealthy during Colonial times. The decor also incorporates her grandparents' fondness for Art Deco. ❋ Casa del Balam is well placed for an investigation of Mérida's merrily pretentious early-twentieth-century buildings and downtown narrow streets, which were originally laid out for horse and buggy traffic. Facing the Opera House and the University of Yucatán, the hotel is close to the lively central plaza and the cathedral. ❋ Isabel Barbachano-Gordon keeps a picture of her revered grandparents beside the reception desk: "My childhood was spent observing my parents and grandmother work continually to improve tourism in the Yucatán," she says. "The promotion and preservation of Mayan culture has always been the core of our family path." ❋

OPPOSITE: Guests enjoy breakfast amid lush palms and the sound of a gently trickling fountain in the Spanish Colonial–style interior courtyard.
ABOVE: The hand-carved wood reception desk blends with the period decor.

RIGHT: Casa del Balam was built in the late 1920s using Spanish Baroque–style construction techniques and period elements. The front entrance is framed with hand-carved *cantera* stone and the door is made of four-inch-thick mahogany and trimmed with antique Spanish brass ornaments.

OPPOSITE, TOP LEFT: The light, airy restaurant features a jaunty Italian black-and-white marble floor.

OPPOSITE, TOP RIGHT: Eighteenth–century porcelain paste tiles line guest room floors. Enormous Art Deco–style stained glass headboards crown the beds.

OPPOSITE, BOTTOM: The palm trees in the interior courtyard are some two-stories tall.

OPPOSITE: A sitting area of comfortable cane-backed cedar rockers adorns the second floor loggia above the interior courtyard.

LEFT: Housed in a wall niche, a Mayan stone figure of a nobleman watches over the pool area.

BELOW: The pleasant backyard pool is surrounded by dense tropical foliage.

❋ HOTEL HACIENDA CHICHÉN

Chichén Itzá, Yucatán

WHILE RUMMAGING THROUGH old family heirlooms recently, Isabel Barbachano-Gordon came across a diary handwritten by her grandmother, Carmen Gomez Rul de Barbachano, more than half a century ago when the family acquired the Hacienda Chichén. It recounts the history of the venerable estate. ❋ Built as a cattle ranch in the sixteenth century, the hacienda's original grounds contained a private chapel where Spanish missionaries tried to convert the Mayan natives to Catholicism. A general store, prison, corrals, and housing for the workers were situated around a large central plaza. Today the main house serves as the hotel's lobby and dining room. ❋ The estate became a sisal plantation during the nineteenth century. In 1900, Edward Herbert Thompson, a Harvard professor and United States vice-consul, bought the hacienda, which included the Mayan archeological wonder Chichén Itzá, for US$75. ❋ Professor Thompson oversaw the dredging of Chichén Itzá's Sacred Well, a *cenote* (limestone pool) two-hundred feet in diameter and one-hundred fifteen feet deep. It yielded a vast collection of offerings: jade, amber, and gold ornaments, knives, copal incense burners, and human bones. Some believe that the *cenote* served as a sacrificial well of Mayan virgins to their rain god, Chac. For the next twenty years, the hacienda served as headquarters for the Carnegie Institute's Maya Archaeological Expedition. ❋ Pioneers in Yucatán tourism, Isabel's grandparents acquired a piece of the property in 1930 and built a hotel on it. Eventually they took over most of the hacienda. It's a mere four-minute walk from the majestic tenth-century temples. In fact, this area is so rich in antiquities that it presents a problem for the hacienda management. Even digging to improve plumbing or to add a new plant to the garden can disturb ruins and might require the hotel to close until the remains have been thoroughly explored. ❋ Since taking over the hotel in 1994, Isabel has worked to restore the hacienda's historic Spanish Colonial ambience. She has decorated the main house with many of her grandparents' belongings, including early photographs of the ruins, reference books, Mayan artifacts, and now, a copy of her grandmother's diary. ❋

OPPOSITE: **A sixteenth-century Colonial landmark, Hacienda Chichén has had many incarnations—it has been a cattle ranch, a sisal plantation, the home of an American vice-consul, the expedition headquarters for teams of archeologists, and finally, a lovely hotel.**
ABOVE: **The original entrance to the hacienda, this arched stone gate leads to grounds verdant with laurels, palms, and orange-blossomed flame-tip trees.**

BELOW: The Yucatán breakfast, enjoyed alfresco by the pool, starts with orange and watermelon juices and fresh-baked sweet breads slathered with butter and wildflower honey, followed by fruit platters and *hojaldras* buns stuffed with cheese and smoked ham or guava fruit paste.

RIGHT: The stone-floored front terrace is dotted with clay pots filled with exotic flora. Rocking chairs were a classic feature of nineteenth-century upper-class Yucatán homes.

OPPOSITE: The sultry jungle climate enables year-round dining on the open-air terrace. The carved cedar shade in the archway is based on an eighteenth-century design.
RIGHT: A statue of San Miguel stands in the living room.
BELOW: In the garden, thick gray palm tree trunks echo the shape and color of old stone pillars and Mayan artifacts.

✳ HOTEL POSADA COATEPEC

IN 1880, HOTEL POSADA COATEPEC manager Justo Fernandez III's great-grandfather sailed from Spain to the New World in search of his brother. He passed through the Veracruz capital Jalapa on his way to Mexico City and fell in love with the warm, mist-shrouded mountainous region. Sadly, he never found his sibling, but he returned to the village of Coatepec, nine miles south of Jalapa, bought an old Spanish Colonial house, and established himself as a coffee grower. ✤ The house and business passed down through the generations. Fernandez explains: "My father was born in the dining room during the Mexican Revolution. There were bullets flying in the streets and it was the only room in the house that didn't have windows." But in the mid-1980s, his father became more interested in horse breeding than coffee growing and decided to turn the four buildings that had been the family home, office, warehouse, and processing plant into a hotel. He renovated the property with an eye for retaining as much of a feeling of the past as possible. The result is a haven of calm, gracious beauty. ✤ Fernandez Junior was charged with designing the Posada's menu. Working with a chef from New York City, he added cosmopolitan flair to traditional Veracruz dishes and Veracruz zest to international ones. For instance, the Italian *caprese* salad comes drizzled with *chipotle* chile dressing, and the light breakfast cottage cheese *enchiladas* are flavored with a distinctive *mole* sauce from the nearby village of Xico, which has a tradition of substituting fruit for the standard chocolate. ✤ From the Posada's roof, one can view the snowcapped peak of Mexico's highest mountain, Pico de Orizaba (18,855 feet), along with a verdant landscape of banana and coffee plantations. ✤

OPPOSITE: The elegant Posada Coatepec is the former villa of a coffee baron. A quaint fountain shaped like a well and adorned with bright flowers bubbles away in the central courtyard.

ABOVE: A gleaming turn-of-the-century buggy parked in the lobby harkens back to the Posada's genteel past. The carriage is a Fernandez family heirloom.

RIGHT: The hotel's Maria Enriqueta Restaurant (named for a celebrated nineteenth-century Veracruz poet), offers innovative cuisine.

OPPOSITE, TOP: The restaurant serves as a gallery for the Fernandez family's extensive collection of Mexican art.

OPPOSITE, BOTTOM: The twenty-four guest rooms, each named after a major city of the world, such as Paris, Venice, and Florence, are individually decorated with a homey array of furnishings. The floors are patterned with original decorative tile and the walls are hand-stenciled with delicate motifs.

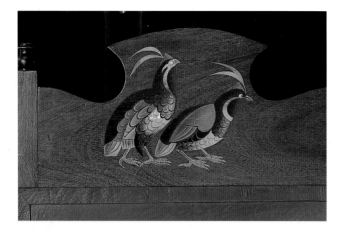

LEFT: Unique hand-painted birds decorate the back of a chair. Lovely acid-etched glass windows create privacy, but still allow light to filter through a guest room door.

BELOW: Arabesques similar to those of Spain's Alhambra are stenciled above the restaurant's doors. Both courtyard and indoor seating are available.

BELOW: The hotel's manager, Justo Fernandez III, an architect, designed the pristine indigo- and white-tiled pool. It is surrounded by stone walkways and flowering vine-covered walls.

❋ MESÓN SACRISTÍA DE LA COMPAÑÍA

Puebla, Puebla

THREE GENERATIONS OF the Espinosa family have been involved in the antiques business, and such was their original motivation for buying this eighteenth-century Puebla house. At least a dozen families had lived in the building by the time they bought it in 1979, so the house itself was a well-used relic in need of much repair. ❋ Once their antiques store opened, things might have continued in their familiar way, but hard times devastated the Mexican economy in the early 1990s, thereby forcing the family to search for an alternative source of income. The Espinosas decided to turn their shop into an inn and restaurant, and they pioneered the concept that almost everything on the premises would be for sale. The project has been a great success; in fact, they are continually having to replace the furniture and dining room plates. ❋ There are only nine guest rooms, each of which is a tasteful gem. With their oak-beamed ceilings and a mix of refined and rustic antiques, you could imagine yourself in a French or Spanish country inn were it not for the sound of live *mariachis* whooping it up downstairs (the management thoughtfully provides earplugs beside each bed for light sleepers). The nightly festivities take place in the cozy bar, which is imaginatively decorated with witty advertising signs from the '50s, vintage musical instruments, and gaily painted fire extinguishers. Bright *papel picado* hand-cut paper banners flutter overhead. ❋ The inn is a showcase for Puebla's Talavera earthenware. In the sixteenth century, the city's potters began basing their work on Spanish majolica designs. Later they incorporated Islamic, Italian, Chinese, and indigenous motifs. The popular hand-painted style appears in many forms today—tableware, tiles, vases, sinks, and even toilets. ❋

OPPOSITE: Swirling wrought-iron gates open to the central courtyard. Suffused with light pouring in from a giant skylight, the burnished orange- and ocher-colored walls seem to glow. ABOVE: Puebla's two-hundred-year-old Mesón Sacristía de la Compañía is both an inn and a fine antiques shop. Nearly everything here—from the long-stemmed wine glasses used at meals to the gilded mirrors in the bathrooms—is for sale.

OPPOSITE: The stylish frog figure at the foot of the bannister is a playful reference to this neighborhood, Plazuela de las Sapos (Toad's Square). The neighborhood grew on the banks of a frog-filled channel that provided water to the nearby Del Carmen Convent.

ABOVE AND RIGHT: Scattered throughout the inn are tables casually laden with *objets d'art.* These treasures provide both a delightful atmosphere and shopping thrills for guests who are so inclined.

BELOW: Bathrooms showcase locally produced Talavera tile.

RIGHT: The centerpiece of the heavenly bridal suite is a genuine Louis XV canopied bed—one of the few items in the inn that's not for sale.

ABOVE: These quirky guest room lamps, forged from an antique typewriter and cash register, spring from the imagination of innkeeper Leobardo Espinosa.

OPPOSITE, TOP: The two double beds in this guest room are brought together with an immense wrought-iron headboard. Exposed brick gives rustic texture to the wall.

OPPOSITE, BOTTOM: The dining room, located in what was formerly the library, has bookshelves lined with antiquarian books.

❋ HACIENDA DE CORTÉS

Cuernavaca, Morelos

LEGEND HAS IT that the conquistador himself, Hernán Cortés, ordered this exquisitely romantic hacienda to be built for his beloved Indian interpreter and lover, Malinche, and that there was a secret tunnel connecting the estate to his palace downtown. ❋ Upon Cortés's death, his son Martin Cortés II, Marques del Valle de Oaxaca, inherited the property, which was then called the Hacienda San Antonio Atlacomulco. In 1848, Lucas Alaman, legal representative to the heirs of the Cortés estate, renovated the hacienda, giving it new life as a sugar plantation. French-imposed Emperor Ferdinand Maximilian is said to have visited the hacienda often. He supposedly delighted in Cuernavaca's beautiful weather before his 1867 execution by firing squad in Querétaro. ❋ Ravaged during the Mexican Revolution, the hacienda was left abandoned. The ruin's next two owners did little to restore it, but in 1973, the estate was acquired by Dr. Mario González Ulloa, a humanitarian surgeon. Dr. Ulloa lovingly reconstructed the property with the advice and assistance of his many artist friends. His sons and sisters carry on the family tradition of arts appreciation by hosting occasional chamber music concerts in the chapel. ❋ Every weekend there are weddings at the hotel, sometimes two or three a day. The ceremonies usually take place on the manicured lawn of the Jardín de Malinche, which is a vast, walled garden whose name keeps the romantic legend alive. The orange-red facades hemming in the lawn are the color that pre-Hispanic civilizations associated with the sunrise and the benevolent gods. ❋

OPPOSITE: At the hotel's entrance, a stone-and-tile fountain overflows exuberantly with flowers.
ABOVE: Many restorations and additions have been made to the Hacienda's structures over the years, with some additions seamlessly grafted on four centuries after the original construction.

TOP: Each guest room has its own private garden terrace outfitted with attractive wrought-iron chairs and Talavera tile–topped tables.

ABOVE: The twenty-two individually decorated two-tiered suites combine stone, tile, plaster, and brick surfaces with comfortable furnishings and original works of art.

RIGHT: On the lawn, a weather-aged wooden cart carries a blooming load of magenta bougainvillea.

OPPOSITE: The restaurant soars up to a ceiling made from the branches of four-hundred-year-old *amate* trees that have grown up inside the stone walls. Lit by candles and wrought-iron chandeliers, this expansive room can seat up to 180 people.

ABOVE: Beyond the terrace's vaulted roof, the brick arches continue, but over the centuries the roof itself crumbled, giving way to the sky.

LEFT: A wall near the pool has nature built right into its structure.
BELOW: The dramatic pool flows around massive stone pillars that once supported a Spanish Colonial roof.
RIGHT: The trickle of this venerable fountain adds to the rich patina of an old red wall.

✻ LAS MAÑANITAS

Cuernavaca, Morelos

THE PROPERTY ACQUIRED its name back in 1932, when a wealthy British expatriate happened to move into the house on his birthday and his friends came around to serenade him with the Mexican birthday song, "Las Mañanitas." But its real vocation became apparent twenty-three years later under the guidance of Robert Krause, a lawyer from Oregon, who fell so heavily under the spell of Cuernavaca that he quit the legal profession and sold all of his belongings to begin a new life south of the border. ✻ He married a young Mexican woman, Margot (who, as his widow, still lives next door), and set about fulfilling his dream of turning Las Mañanitas into a sophisticated small hotel and restaurant modeled after the Relais & Châteaux resorts of Europe. ✻ "We had a new business and we didn't know anything about it," recalls manager Ruben Cerda, who began as a busboy one month after the restaurant opened. In the beginning, it was such a shoestring operation that they had to discreetly remove cups and saucers from the table as soon as they were empty and then hurriedly wash and dry them to serve new customers. ✻ Krause hired an English teacher to give lessons to the twelve-person staff every morning. After a few years, he sent Cerda to Italy and France to study hotels: "I learned everything from him. He was a second father to me," says Cerda, who now manages a staff of 140. ✻ The guest room furniture was custom made, but the overall interior design evolved gradually. "When you do decor," says Cerda, "it is like a painting, and when an artist begins, he doesn't know exactly how he's going to finish. You have to feel what you are doing." The Aztecs called Cuernavaca the "City of Eternal Spring," and indeed this is a place where dinner is invariably savored by candlelight in the garden under the stars. Cerda fondly remembers that when anyone used to ask Robert Krause what Las Mañanitas really meant, he would answer: "I think it's love." ✻

OPPOSITE: A flock of noble African cranes shares the grounds with peacocks and pink flamingos. *ABOVE:* Before dinner, guests congregate on the garden patio for cocktails and watch the peacocks do their humorous dance.

ABOVE: The pool garden slopes down to a shallow pond where the exotic birds feed.

RIGHT: Bordering the swimming pool are giant clay pots overflowing with bougainvillea. Overhead a *clavellino* tree, with its pink flowers, stands opposite two towering palm trees.

ABOVE: The hotel's restaurant is world renowned for its gracious service and sublime Mexican and Continental cuisine. Note the peacock motif on the dishes.

OPPOSITE, TOP: Based on a Spanish Colonial design, the beautifully proportioned bar was hand-carved by a local craftsman. Las Mañanitas bartenders are well trained in the art of the margarita.

OPPOSITE, BOTTOM: Puebla Talavera tiles dating back to 1934 grace the dining room fireplace.

RIGHT: The hotel's north-wing hallway floor is made of multihued polished stone. Tall candlesticks, Talavera vases, pew benches, ceramic pots, and a vintage carousel horse adorn the hallway.

OPPOSITE, TOP LEFT: A carved cherub tops a *cantera* stone archway.

OPPOSITE, TOP RIGHT: Ginger jars from Puebla glazed in the blue and white "folded napkin" Talavera pattern.

OPPOSITE, BOTTOM: These three copper pots are from Santa Clara del Cobre.

LEFT: The twenty-two guest suites have carved Spanish Baroque headboards, hand-woven white area rugs, and sofas covered with Schiaparelli pink upholstery and accented with lime green throw pillows.
RIGHT: Fireplaces create a romantic ambience in the patio and garden suites.

❋ POSADA DEL TEPOZTECO

LOCATED TWELVE MILES northeast of Cuernavaca, Tepoztlán is the mythical birthplace, more than twelve hundred years ago, of Quetzalcóatl, the all-powerful serpent god of the Aztecs. Believing it to be a spiritual power spot, the Aztecs constructed a thirty-three foot high temple on a cliff above the village. The Pyramid of Tepozteco is dedicated to Tepoztécatl, the god of fertility and *pulque* (a ceremonial alcoholic beverage made from the maguey cactus). ❋ To this day, the Nahuatl-speaking villagers revere Tepoztécatl because when the Spanish conquerors flung the idol off the cliff, the villagers found that it had landed unscathed. Every year on September 7, the community celebrates El Reto del Tepozteco, a raucous fiesta during which they toast to the god's resilience with copious shots of *pulque*. ❋ The Posada del Tepozteco was built in the 1930s as a rustic weekend getaway for an artistic family from Mexico City. The original house didn't have electricity. It became a hotel in the 1950s, one of the first in the village. Alejandro Camarena took over the property in 1994. Explaining his concept for the inn, Camarena says, "In the new millennium everybody is a number. Here at the Posada del Tepozteco we don't want mega-luxury, rather we want to make a simple, pampering atmosphere where people feel like individuals, not numbers." ❋ His first step toward creating such a peaceful environment was to remove the television from the bar, replacing the rowdy soccer matches with the soothing sound of classical music. He revamped the menu to include organic vegetables and light sauces in addition to traditional hearty Mexican fare. He renovated the estate utilizing ecological principles, including the installation of solar heaters, tanks to catch rainwater, and a gray water—recycling system for the garden. ❋ There is a dome-shaped *temezcal*, which is an indiginous sweat lodge made of adobe and stone. Camarena describes the *temezcal* experience as being "like rebirth." He says, "First you are in the round, humid, warm atmosphere, then you are born into the cold air and light. You bathe in running water, then you bundle up and rest." ❋

OPPOSITE: The spectacular eastward view takes in the valley of Tepotzlán and the sixteenth-century church and former convent Dominico de la Natividad.
ABOVE: A lush canopy of mixed magenta, red, and orange bougainvillea provides shade on the outdoor dining/cocktail terrace.

BELOW: This covered seating area frames the mountain view with tall stone arches. The *equipal* (leather and wood) couch sits easily with a seventeenth-century trunk used as a coffee table.

RIGHT: The relaxed tone of the lobby bar is set by a twelve-by-six-foot pastoral Indian scene painted by esteemed local artist Gustavo Montoya.

LEFT: A dining room hutch is filled with hand-lacquered ceramic dishes from the state of Guerrero. Each dish depicts various tasty-looking Mexican breads, fruits, and vegetables.
ABOVE: The cheery restaurant has a vaulted brick ceiling and fanciful borders painted around the picture windows.

OPPOSITE, TOP AND ABOVE: There are two solar-heated pools on the property, one behind the rose garden and the other close to the new two-story wing designed by architect/manager Alejandro Camarena.

OPPOSITE, BOTTOM: A classic Spanish-style courtyard fountain is tucked in among orange trees and blooming birds of paradise.

❋ HOTEL CAMINO REAL OAXACA

Oaxaca, Oaxaca

A NATIONAL HERITAGE SITE, the Hotel Camino Real Oaxaca occupies the premises of the former Santa Catalina Convent. Under the auspices of Dominican friar Bernardo de Albuquerque, the building broke ground on February 12, 1576. The Spanish friar spent most of his life mastering the dialect of the Zapotec people and evangelizing them. According to the hotel's pamphlet, the friar constructed the convent on his own land with the aim of receiving "poor and virtuous girls who wished to devote their life to God as nuns." Eventually this group numbered 401 novices, who learned manual labor skills, Latin, singing, and religious rituals. ❋ The convent closed in 1862 as a result of Benito Juárez's Reform Laws, which mandated the nationalism of Church property. The convent was occupied in turn by the city government, a municipal jail, an art school, a Masonic lodge, and a cinema before its conversion into a hotel in 1975. ❋ Wherever possible, the hotel's restoration crew left surfaces in their natural state—cracked plaster revealing original stones as reminders of the venerable age of the building. Great effort was made to restore as much of the building's decorative glory as possible. Treasured religious canvases, some replicas but many originals, line the cool stone corridors and hang above the beds. Recordings of Gregorian chants echo throughout the courtyards at breakfast time. ❋ The convent's public rooms have retained their old names. Las Novicias, once the convent's library and still lined with archaic religious texts, is now a bar. The former refectory, El Refectorio, serves as a lovely alfresco dining area. The chapel, La Capilla, is a buffet restaurant capable of accommodating up to five hundred people. The hotel hosts a crafts market and weekly folk dance extravaganza at the chapel, which includes the famous Oaxacan "Pineapple Dance." The indigenous dancers wear wildly colorful costumes of lace, silk, and velvet, cascades of glittering necklaces, and splendid feather headdresses. ❋ Oaxaca offers some of Mexico's finest shopping for folk art. Among the crafts available are the region's distinctive black pottery, tin ornaments and mirrors, hand-loomed rugs, embroidered clothing, lacquer-painted gourds, carved wooden creatures, and replicas of the pre-Hispanic gold earrings found at the nearby Zapotec ruin, Monte Albán. ❋

OPPOSITE: Housed in a four-hundred-year-old former convent, the Hotel Camino Real Oaxaca is a place of secluded courtyards, secret patios, and jasmine-scented gardens.
ABOVE: A shrine to the Virgin resides in a wall niche.

ABOVE: Room keys come on strands of rosary beads, but the ninety-one rooms, decorated with hand-painted frescoes, vibrant orange bedspreads, magenta pillows, and discreet mini-bars, are a far cry from the monastic cells from which they originated.

OPPOSITE, TOP: The second-floor walkway surrounding the principal courtyard is lined with bougainvillea, geraniums, and lantana.

OPPOSITE, BOTTOM: Throughout the hotel, subtly hued retouched and original frescoes cast a peaceful spell.

OPPOSITE, TOP AND BOTTOM: Originally the convent's washing area, Los Lavaderos is an ingeniously designed octagonal fountain that flows into a dozen carved-stone troughs. Now the charming spot is a popular site for weddings.

LEFT: This burnished black-clay statue of a Oaxacan *señorita* welcomes guests to the hotel's elegant dining room, El Refectorio.

✳ CASA DE ESPÍRITUS ALEGRES

Marfil, Guanajuato

THERE ARE SKELETONS literally in every closet at the Casa de Espíritus Alegres (House of the Happy Spirits). Called *calaveras*, these merry cadavers are created by Mexican folk artists in celebration of the Day of the Dead. Some guests find the wood, papier-mâché, and clay sculptures unnerving, but in Mexico, death isn't morbid. As Octavio Paz wrote in *The Labyrinth of Solitude*, "The Mexican is familiar with death, jokes about it, caresses it, sleeps with it, celebrates it; it is one of his favorite toys and his most steadfast love."[1] The skeleton imagery keeps the memory of deceased loved ones alive. It also prompts people to remember their own mortality and, it is hoped, to treasure life more deeply as a result. ✳ Two miles from downtown Guanajuato, the B&B's lovely two-story stone building dates back to the 1700s, when it was a part of the Hacienda la Trinidad, a silver processing plant. A 1906 flood destroyed much of the estate, and it remained virtually abandoned until the 1950s, when Italian sculptor Giorgio Belloli began restoring and creating homes out of the ruined hacienda. Joan and Carol Summers, artists from California, bought the house in 1979. Initially the building was their studio, but as more and more friends began visiting, it gradually became an inn. ✳ Joan, who passed away in 1998, was a passionate folk art collector who was dedicated to climbing mountains, fording rivers, and wandering down desolate, dusty roads in search of soulful treasures. She once bought an extra seat on an airplane flight just to accommodate one of her finds. The house now showcases crafts from every state in Mexico alongside equally colorful tapestries and puppets from the Rajasthan region of India. ✳ Many of its delightful items are for sale in an informal shop off the downstairs patio. The ever-changing stock ranges from mischievous-eyed devil figures that get blown to bits with fireworks as part of the Mexican Easter to classy silver necklaces to kitsch Virgin of Guadalupe nightlights. In the charmingly explicit house rules handed to every guest, the casa's kindhearted manager, Betsy McNair, recommends the store as twenty-four-hour retail therapy. "Can't sleep?" she asks. "Shop! You are welcome to browse at your leisure. Items you select to purchase may be taken to your room and we can settle up when you check out." ✳

1. Octavio Paz, *The Labyrinth of Solitude.* (New York: Grove Press, 1961).

OPPOSITE AND ABOVE: **Casa de Espíritus Alegres is a paradise for lovers of folk art. Among the treasures in the living room are a tiger mask from Chiapas, tall wooden standards carried in Oaxacan Easter processions, and a top-hatted papier-mâché skeleton street cleaner made by Mexico City's famous Linares Brothers.**

OPPOSITE: A red Judas figure and a giant papier-mâché skeleton dangle festively from the rafters. The canary yellow of the woodwork and window trim paired with the indigo and white of the zigzag tiles is a classic color combination found in many traditional Mexican kitchens.

LEFT: The late Joan Summers's nutty sense of humor still permeates the house. Here in the dining room, she used to put party dresses on the skeletons.

BELOW: The breakfast table is always a surprise at Casa de Espíritus Alegres. Depending on the innkeeper's mood, you might find it decked with a wild fruit-patterned tablecloth, or one emblazoned with a hundred grinning skulls, or a glittering cover made of gold lamé.

ABOVE: A timeworn shuttered door
and pink *cantera* stone columns
topped with leafy capitals form the
whimsical entry to the Casita de Betsy.

OPPOSITE, TOP: Everyday plastic plates
and scrubbers become artful objects
against the tomato-red wall.

OPPOSITE, BOTTOM: Colors dazzle the
eyes in the Casita de Betsy. The black
appliquéd bedspread is from India;
the hand-woven red floor rug is from
Pátzcuaro.

RIGHT: A woodcut by Carol Summers enlivens the sitting area of the Las Muñecas room.

OPPOSITE: Each of the eight bedrooms has a distinctive theme. The decor of El Quetzal was inspired by the gorgeous plumage of the near-extinct *quetzal* bird. A Huichol Indian yarn painting hangs above the colorful bed, and festive *papel picado* banners flutter overhead.

ABOVE: This bathroom is an inspired crazy quilt of Talavera tiles from Dolores Hidalgo.

OPPOSITE: This custom-made bathroom sink features lighthearted skeletons designed by Joan Summers. This signature pattern also appears on the inn's coffee mugs and dinner plates. The tin mirror is from San Miguel de Allende.

ABOVE: The inn's Edenic garden feels
a world away from the busy road on
the other side of the high wall.

LEFT: The upper wall is painted *azul añil*, which is a deep ultramarine blue believed to protect against evil spirits.
BELOW: The arched front door is framed by intricate *cantera* stonework.

89

✳ CASA DE SIERRA NEVADA

San Miguel de Allende, Guanajuato

SAN MIGUEL DE ALLENDE is a national historic landmark 160 miles northwest of Mexico City that is governed by strict preservation codes. The downtown area's narrow cobblestone streets, free of neon signs and traffic lights, still look much as they did when the town was founded some 450 years ago. Often described as a resort without a beach, the high-desert (6,400 feet) destination is a favorite weekend getaway for residents of Mexico City. ✳ Since the 1940s, San Miguel has also accommodated a substantial community of expatriates. After World War II, the GI Bill enabled many veterans to travel to Mexico to study art at the Instituto Allende. These days the expat population, estimated to be about three thousand strong, is predominantly composed of retirees from Canada and the United States. They come for the temperate weather, the abundance of English-language cultural events, and to live far more luxurious lifestyles than their pensions would afford at home. Many are active volunteers for local charitable organizations that provide social services, educational services, and health-care resources to the needy. ✳ The Casa de Sierra Nevada encompasses ten Spanish Colonial mansions, all within walking distance of the central square. The original house on Calle Hospicio was built in 1580 as the home of a silver tycoon. The building became the residence of the bishop of Guanajuato in the eighteenth century. In the 1950s, Jorge Palomino, Marquis de Sierra Nevada, restored the property and, by incorporating several adjoining buildings, turned it into an inn. Current owner James Sprowls acquired the property in 1994. He modernized the facilities while maintaining the historic ambience, and his Spanish-born wife, Marta Villanueva, handled the decor. She commissioned antique-style furnishings made in Dolores Hidalgo and adorned the suites with regional crafts. ✳ The hotel's principal restaurant, with its classical guitarist and dishes such as steamed mussels in white wine with saffron cream, is more formal than most establishments in San Miguel. To ensure a refined dining experience, the management requires that guests be at least sixteen years of age and that men wear dinner jackets. ✳ The beauty spa specializes in aromatherapy massages and herbal wraps. You can pamper your body with Moroccan rose-petal extract, Chinese green tea, algae clay, and lemon essence. Treatments are administered either inside or up on the spa's garden roof terrace. ✳ "This is a guest house," says Swiss-born manager Markus Oderman. "We want the inn to feel like a private home. If it feels like a hotel we've failed." ✳

OPPOSITE: This tranquil interior courtyard is surrounded by guest rooms. The sparkling fountain is decorated with flamboyant blue-and-white zigzag tiles.
ABOVE: A striking ceramic urn from Dolores Hidalgo anchors this white staircase.

ABOVE: Tables in the patio dining area take a folkloric turn with black ceramic candleholders from Oaxaca.

RIGHT: Adorning the wall of the patio dining area is an eighteenth-century Gobelin tapestry.

OPPOSITE: The meticulous hand-stenciled walls in the Lace Room Bar are a replica of those found in the eighteenth-century Sanctuary de Jesus Nazareno de Atontonilco, which is a half-hour drive from San Miguel de Allende.

OPPOSITE: The most recent addition to the hotel, the Casa de Sierra Nevada en el Parque, located in a former hacienda at the crest of Juárez Park, has just five exclusive guest rooms.

LEFT: The hotel's private swimming pool is flanked by ancient stone colonnades.

BELOW: This dining area is located under the *portales* adjacent to the swimming pool.

LEFT: A gleaming copper sink is set in among translucent-glazed blue tiles.
BELOW: The Lemon Room features an oil still life by Sonoran artist Gustavo Valenzuela.
OPPOSITE: Wicker furniture appoints this quiet patio near the main restaurant.

❋ CASA LUNA B&B

San Miguel de Allende, Guanajuato

CASA LUNA TRANSLATES as "Moon House," but when Dianne Kushner, a former psychotherapist from California, impulsively bought the two-hundred-year-old property back in 1994, her friends teased her that "luna" must mean "lunatic." They thought she was nuts to invest her life savings in such a dilapidated wreck, but where they saw rubble, she saw the house's "great bones" and how its rambling layout was potentially ideal for a bed and breakfast inn. Kushner explains: "I named the house Luna because the moon is a feminine symbol and indicates change, as in the phases of the moon and cycles—and this move was a big change for me." In 1993, four friends of hers died within a six-month period, causing her to realize that life is short. So she bought a '78 Blazer four-wheel-drive truck and headed south in search of adventure. She left her family, friends, and business behind, but had no regrets. ❋ After an intensive ten-month restoration effort, the B&B opened with just four rooms. An ongoing project, the house now has nine airy guest rooms, each with a fireplace and private little patio. Kushner took full advantage of the structure's many nooks and crannies by filling the house with an intriguing array of treasures from San Miguel's antique bazaars and artisan workshops. ❋ The overall effect is utterly romantic. As one traveler wrote in the guest book, "I always wanted to sleep in a bed where the pillows took up more space than I did." Another remarked, "I'll remember the sound of the fountain, the crickets, and the aroma of the honeysuckle." ❋

OPPOSITE: **A flagstone path meanders through archways connecting the plant-filled central courtyards.**
ABOVE: **One of three fountains in the house, this pretty shell-shaped one stands in the front patio.**

ABOVE: These painted tin *nichos* filled with humorous and poignant Day of the Dead imagery were made in San Miguel de Allende.

RIGHT: The delightful Frida Kahlo Room is filled with Mexican folk art, including coconut masks from Guerrero, lacquered wooden plates from Michoacán, and papier-mâché dolls from Celaya.

OPPOSITE: In the Red Room is a spectacular pairing of a blue, polished cement floor with walls washed a luminous Pompeii red. A locally made tin fixture hangs from the lofty *bóveda* (vaulted) brick ceiling.

RIGHT, TOP: These brass fixtures and hand-blown glass pitcher set were made in San Miguel de Allende.

RIGHT, BOTTOM: Dianne Kushner spent months casually accruing "imperfect" seconds from Dolores Hidalgo tile factories. When the time finally came to tile, she sat down with her *maestro* and together they improvised this uniquely splendid bathroom.

OPPOSITE: Guests unwind in the Garden Room's smoky blue, polished cement tub surrounded by soft candlelight, ferns, and vines.

ABOVE: This kitchen showcases an assortment of Talavera tiles and vases from Dolores Hidalgo, alongside wacky ceramic chickens from Santa Cruz de las Huertas, Jalisco, and bright tin ones from San Miguel de Allende.

RIGHT: In 1999, Dianne Kushner bought the chicken farm next door to build a grand new dining room needed to accommodate her increasing number of guests. The large mirrored tapestry is from India.

✽ LA CASA DE LA MARQUESA

Querétaro, Querétaro

ACCORDING TO THE LEGEND, in 1756 a Spanish nobleman named El Marques de la Villa del Villar del Águila fell in love with a nun of the Franciscan Order of St. Clare. Supposedly she declined his advances, but she asked of him two favors: (1) that he build an aqueduct to bring water to the people of Querétaro, and (2) that he construct the most beautiful house in the city. The marquis instructed his executor, Don Juan Antonio de Urrutia y Arana, to build a small Baroque palace in her honor. Eventually the residence was occupied by Don Juan's wife, Josefina Paula Guerrero y Davila, but rumors persist to this day that a tunnel once connected the mansion's cellar to the nearby convent. ✽ The city of Querétaro has played an important role in Mexican history. In 1810, the first plans for independence from Spain were conspired at the home of Josefa Ortiz de Domínguez, who happened to be the mayor's wife. In 1848, the Mexican-American War concluded in Querétaro with the signing of the Treaty of Guadalupe. Emperor Maximilian made his last stand here before a firing squad in 1867, and in 1917 the city served as the site for the signing of the Mexican Constitution, which remains the basis of Mexican law today. ✽ After decades of neglect, La Casa de la Marquesa was restored to its original grandeur in 1995 by hotel owner Carmelita González de Cosío de Urquiza. No stranger to history herself (both her father and great-grandfather served as governors of Querétaro), she decided to name each of the twenty-five guest rooms (fourteen in the original mansion, eleven in a neighboring building) after a key figure from Mexican and Spanish history and literature. For instance, the Iturbide Room was named for the ambitious Creole colonel Agustín de Iturbide, who actually stayed at the casa in 1847. A royalist who defected to join the rebels during Mexico's fight for independence, Iturbide became the first emperor of the independent government. Other suites were named for Don Quixote; Maximilian and his wife, Carlota; and Cristóbal Colón (Christopher Columbus). ✽

OPPOSITE AND ABOVE: **Built in 1757, La Casa de la Marquesa is a gem of Moorish Baroque architecture.**

ABOVE: Fine reproductions of historic European paintings and tapestries add to the hotel's aristocratic atmosphere.
RIGHT: The Alhambra Room is decorated in the Morosco (Arabian) style; an exceptional, intricately carved and painted wooden panel with decorative leaded-glass windows separates the bedroom from the bathroom.
OPPOSITE: Sunlight filters through lace curtains into a guest room. The polished mahogany floor is covered with a Persian rug.

BELOW: Light pours in through a concave, diamond-shaped skylight to the central courtyard below. The palm is potted in a rotund copper vase from China.

RIGHT AND OPPOSITE: Gently scalloped stone steps lead to the small chapel. The risers are decorated with fine tiles from Puebla. A stained-glass Virgin of Guadalupe glows behind the altar.

RIGHT: The Café Real is located in the central courtyard of the hotel's annex building, the Casa Azul.
OPPOSITE: Niches filled with beautiful Talavera urns adorn the stairway leading from the café to guest rooms.

❊ CASA VIEJA

IT'S NOT EASY TO FIND an ancient building in Mexico City's swank Polanco district, where the city's elite dwell in palatial apartments tended by bevies of servants. Casa Vieja (Old House) comes as something of a surprise. At first glance, the house appears to be falling down in front of your eyes. Closer inspection, however, reveals the structure to be a brilliant stage set. Built as a private residence in the 1940s, the building's crumbling facade is a meticulously maintained illusion. ❊ The house belongs to Mexican newscaster Lolita Ayala. She was in fact born in what is now the Presidential Suite. In the early 1990s, Ayala and her former husband, Luis Sosa, decided to convert the property into a small hotel. They wanted to combine the traditional rich colors and warmth of Mexican style with advanced technology and European comfort. ❊ The ten suites, named for acclaimed Mexican cultural figures such as Frida Kahlo, Rufino Tamayo, and Agustín Lara, are the essence of luxurious practicality, with blenders, microwave ovens, televisions, VCRs, sound systems, phone and fax machines, Jacuzzis, and saunas. Even the pencil holders and ashtrays were specially designed to harmonize with the decor. ❊ Polanco is just north of Chapultepec Park. The vast park provides a welcome refuge for the urban populace. It contains gardens, boating lakes, sports fields, a zoo, and several museums, including the marvelous Museum of Anthropology. ❊

OPPOSITE: From the street, Casa Vieja looks like an aesthetically deteriorating centuries-old hacienda, but in fact it was built as a private home in the 1940s. This illusion is created with roughly cut stone and a watery, layered faux-paint finish.
ABOVE: An extraordinary green and purple color scheme enlivens the Presidential Suite.

RIGHT: The foyer has the feel of a medieval hallway. Its Moorish-patterned frescoes curve around the barrel-vaulted roof. On the beveled glass table are candles and images of Mexico's beloved Virgin of Guadalupe.

OPPOSITE, LEFT: Throughout the hotel, the walls are stained luminous colors using pre-Hispanic-style dyes rendered from natural substances such as roots, seeds, insects, flowers, minerals, and rocks. These stairs go to Casa Lola, the Presidential Suite.

OPPOSITE, RIGHT: The view from the stairs looking into the courtyard. The carved wooden window-box planters were made by a Michoacán craftsman.

OPPOSITE: The rooftop bar is brightened by a tiled painting copied from Diego Rivera's famous work *Los Alcatraces* (*The Calla Lilies*).

LEFT: In the restaurant, a prize-winning Tolucan six-by-four-foot "Tree of Life" sculpture portrays the story of humanity from Adam's rib to the Last Judgment.

BELOW: A loosely thatched bamboo roof shades the rooftop restaurant. *Equipal* (leather and wood) chairs, yellow tablecloths set off by blue cloth napkins, and handblown polka dot glassware create an amiable setting to enjoy such house specialites as red snapper topped with melon salsa or sweet and sour shrimp in coconut sauce.

OPPOSITE, TOP: The suites are named after renowned Mexican artists and celebrities. This one pays tribute to composer Agustín Lara. Artist Mauricio Galguera was commissioned to paint portraits of all the honorees on the kitchenette refrigerators.

OPPOSITE, BOTTOM: This bedroom in the Presidential Suite features a beautiful bed incorporating slim wrought-iron tree branches. A custom-made bedspread appliquéd with leaf shapes complements the bed's tree theme.

LEFT: Sumptuous fabrics, spirited folk art, and vibrant colors combine to give each suite its own unique personality. Here a deeply hued bedspread and matching canopy are appliquéd with brilliant satin ribbons.

ABOVE: The David Alfaro Siqueiros Room, named for the revered muralist, has a lemon-yellow bedspread. The walls and plastered *bóveda* (vaulted) ceiling are washed a radiant yellow with a sky blue trim.

✽ VILLA MONTAÑA

Morelia, Michoacán

WHEN PHILIPPE DE REISET, a French count, first arrived in Morelia nearly thirty years ago, he was fresh from tending his family's banana and rice plantation in Ecuador and planned to seek out a ranch in Mexico. But when he discovered the Villa Montaña for sale, he decided to buy it, and he and his wife, Eva, began to prowl Mexico's antiques bazaars and regional crafts markets in search of goods to fill their forty-three guest cottages. Still an avid shopper, de Reiset says, "When we find something we like, we store it until we can incorporate it into the right surrounding. Any find, from a column to a piece of tile, can inspire a change in a room." ✾ Located halfway between Mexico City and Guadalajara, Morelia is the capital of the state of Michoacán. Founded in 1541, the stately Spanish Colonial city is a UNESCO World Heritage Site. It is also the candy capital of Mexico. At the Mercado de Dulces (market of sweets) you can sample all sorts of local confections, including *ate* (a candied guava or mango paste), *cajeta* (heavenly caramel sauce made from goat milk), and *rompope* (an indigenous eggnog). ✾ The Purépecha Indian communities of Lake Pátzcuaro are an hour's drive away. Each lakeside village specializes in a particular folk art. Santa Clara del Cobre is famous for its copperware, Tzintzuntzan for its straw creations and ceramics, and Tocuaro for its carved wooden masks. Pátzcuaro is known for its lacquerware and hand-loomed textiles, Santa Cruz for its embroidered scenes of village life, and Quiroga for its brightly painted wooden toys. ✾ The writer Jorge Luis Borges once stayed at the Villa Montaña while attending a poetry festival in Morelia. Old and blind, he told his companion, "This hotel is very pretty." His companion said, "How can you say so, Borges, if you cannot see?" He replied, "Because it smells of roses." ✾

OPPOSITE: Nestled in the Santa Maria hills above Morelia, the Villa Montaña has all the trappings of a wealthy Mexican estate. Its four impeccably groomed acres are filled with colorful flowers year-round.

ABOVE: This eighteenth-century Spanish Colonial door leads to the owners' suite.

ABOVE: Brick pathways wind under ivy-cloaked archways, past stone fountains, and through sweet patios.
RIGHT: A menagerie of locally carved stone sculptures sits on the brick staircase in front of the restaurant.

ABOVE AND OPPOSITE, TOP: Guests can dine alfresco under the *portales* or inside the formal dining room.

OPPOSITE, BOTTOM: In the lobby, plush white couches surround a coffee table made from a thick antique door. An eighteenth-century painting of the Virgin of Guadalupe hangs above the fireplace flanked by two Talavera ginger jars on the mantle.

❊ CASA LUNA

Zihuatanejo, Guerrero

ZIHUATANEJO IS REPUTED to have been a royal bathing resort for the Tarascan Indians during pre-Hispanic times. Located 150 miles northwest of Acapulco, this sleepy fishing village has always attracted a certain kind of discerning visitor. John Wayne and the Hollywood crowd discovered it in the 1940s when they came to fish and shoot jaguar and boar. In the 1960s, it was in the news again when Timothy Leary established a dropout base here for his International Foundation for Internal Freedom. ❊ Joe and Patsy LoGiudice were veterans of the New York City art scene (Joe worked as an art dealer and Patsy made documentary films) when they bought Casa Luna in 1972. Back then, it was dingy four-room concrete hut. A trained architect, Joe found the challenge irresistible and together with a group of friends that included '60s radical Abbie Hoffman, *Louisville Courier-Journal* heiress Eleanor Bingham, and painter Larry Rivers, he set to work transforming the site into his personal bohemian Shangri-la. ❊ Viewing the house as "an ongoing sculpture," they worked with natural materials to create rooms that remain open to the elements as much as possible. The soaring *palapa* roof is composed of thick layers of palm thatch that reflect the sun and offer insulation from the heat. It took four-acres' worth of palms to provide enough thatch for the huge roof. ❊ In addition to the main house, there are four adobe bungalows painted pretty Mexican shades of cobalt, lavender, and turquoise. At first, sand floors seemed appropriate for the buildings, but soon there were frogs, and then snakes arrived to eat the frogs, and then a mongoose came to prey on the snakes, so finally they covered the ground with local *bara* tiles. ❊

OPPOSITE: A fountain sits at the entrance to the house. The large garden is a tropical Eden teeming with orchids, ferns, hibiscus, papayas, and mangoes.
ABOVE: New York painter Larry Rivers uses this studio cottage as a winter retreat. Rivers says Zihuatanejo is "like dropping out in paradise, practically like Gauguin."

ABOVE: A sleeping loft is tucked into the *palapa* roof of the main house. Aerodynamically designed to withstand the occasional hurricane, the roof is composed of thick layers of palm thatch and hand-hewn *bacoté* hardwood beams.

RIGHT: The sea breeze blows through the indoor/outdoor living room, which sits just eighty yards above Playa la Ropa beach.

✻ CASAS DE CAREYES

Costa Careyes, Jalisco

ON JULY 2, 1968, Gian Franco Brignone was flying in a single-engine plane between Puerto Vallarta and Manzanillo when he saw a rocky coastline dotted with hidden bays and thought it the most beautiful place on earth. He set off on horseback to explore the terrain. Now 74, he remembers, "There were no roads. I had to open the way with a machete. It was as perfect as an angel's wing." ✻ Heir to an Italian banking fortune, Brignone proceeded to acquire six thousand acres and enlisted the services of French architect Jean-Claude Galibert, who in turn drew inspiration from the bold minimalist designs of Mexican architect Luis Barragán. Galibert, however, eschewed the master's hard-edged right angles in favor of soft Mediterranean curves. Taking full advantage of the balmy microclimate (it usually rains just twenty days a year), Galibert designed the open-air structures to take advantage of the sunlight and sea breeze. ✻ The resort now encompasses Casitas de las Flores (a pueblo-style condominium development), Villas de Careyes (thirty-five spectacular cliff-top houses), Jardínes de Playa Rosa (four villas on a private beach), a health spa, a French-Mexican restaurant, and a polo club. Brignone designated the rest of the estate as a nature reserve to protect the endangered native turtles called *careyes*. Between July and October the turtles lay their eggs at night on Teopa Beach. Six to ten weeks later, the babies hatch, dig their way out of the sand, and bumble into the waves. ✻

OPPOSITE: All of the accommodations at Casas de Careyes, including the private villas and *casitas*, are managed like hotels with a full maid service. Guests may choose to have meals catered or groceries delivered to cook in their private kitchens.
ABOVE: The playful paint jobs are unforgettable—every wall reveals a radiant color.

ABOVE: Just off the terrace, with a stunning ocean view, this *casita* living room is sunny and warm. The lizard design painted on a ceremonial drum continues to dance up and over the wall.

OPPOSITE, TOP: At Casas de Careyes, all buildings face the sea. Designed for maximum privacy, the architecture ensures that no one sees directly into neighboring units.

OPPOSITE, BOTTOM LEFT: A little painting of a parrot indicates the name of a room.

OPPOSITE, BOTTOM RIGHT: A bronze fish fountain graces the front of a purple-blue *casita*.

EL PERICO

OPPOSITE: Eleven guests fit easily
around the large *equipal* dining table
in the Casa Sol de Oriente (Sun
House of the East).
ABOVE: These shocking pink, shaggy
palapa-roofed *casitas* sparkle next to
a green lawn.

BELOW: White gauze mosquito netting covers a bed on the terrace.

RIGHT: This seating area made of molded pink cement is softened with white cushions and scores of throw pillows. The rug underfoot is actually a mosaic made of pebbles.

OPPOSITE: A moat-shaped pool borders the Casa Sol de Oriente. On the other side of the bay, a twin pool surrounds the Casa Sol de Occidente. These two six-bedroom houses are identical, differing only in ornamentation.

ABOVE: Casa Sol de Occidente (Sun House of the West) features an airy, open floor plan.

RIGHT: Brilliant yellow pillows contrast with a purple couch and rich red walls.

OPPOSITE: Casas de Careyes properties enjoy panoramic ocean views.

❋ LAS ALAMANDAS

Costalegre, Jalisco

NESTLED INTO A fifteen-hundred-acre ecological reserve encompassing palm-fringed beaches, freshwater lagoons, and tropical jungles, Las Alamandas is a two-hour drive from Manzanillo or Puerto Vallarta, but many visitors choose to arrive by Learjet on the resort's private landing strip. ❋ The Pacific Coast property was bought in 1980 by Bolivian tin king Don Antenor Patiño, who founded the celebrated Las Hadas resort in Manzanillo in the mid-1960s. He had even grander plans for the Las Alamandas tract but managed only to clear a network of dirt roads before his death. His granddaughter, Isabel Goldsmith, who inherited the property, had very different ideas about developing the land. Rather than build a mega-hotel with thousands of rooms, she decided to create an exclusive luxury hideaway. ❋ She opened her retreat in 1990 with five villas and has since added one more. Even when all six villas are occupied, guests rarely catch sight of one another unless they happen to turn up in the bar or restaurant at the same time. ❋ Upon arrival, the manager asks guests what level of attention they desire. Service can be highly solicitous—a white-shirted attendant checking in every thirty minutes—or it can be invisible, with preordered cocktails silently left on your doorstep at dusk. Pretty much any reasonable request is granted. The most popular requests are to fly in a *mariachi* band from Puerto Vallarta to accompany a birthday bash and to reserve a mile-long stretch of beach for a romantic candlelit dinner. ❋ Among the outdoor activities are horseback riding, mountain biking, hiking, fishing, snorkeling, bird-watching, taking boat rides on the San Nicolás River, and, of course, eating chocolate-covered tequila bonbons by the pool. ❋

OPPOSITE: One of six beachfront villas, the Casa del Domo, with its high, pink dome, is sequestered behind towering coconut palms, thick bougainvillea, and an extravagant cactus garden.
ABOVE: Multihued steps are painted hot pink, avocado, yellow, and Mediterranean blue-green.

OPPOSITE, TOP: Hand-painted tables in the shade are a pleasant spot for lunch or a leisurely game of cards.

OPPOSITE, BOTTOM: The dining room serves gourmet fare using fresh seafood and organic fruits, vegetables, and herbs grown in the estate's orchards and gardens.

ABOVE: Designed by owner Isabel Goldsmith, the villas are decorated in ebullient, fiesta-like colors: orangey pinks, mint greens, yellows, pale blues. In addition, all of the villas are open to the sea. The floors are patterned with mosaics of smooth stones.

LEFT: The sixty-foot pool, complete
with pulsating massage jets, is surrounded by fashionable chaise
longues and pergolas.

ABOVE: A fringed white hammock
that is large enough for two swings
in an outdoor living room.

RIGHT: In an interior courtyard, a fern
takes center stage framed by a yellow arch and a blue wall.

RIGHT: The Casa del Domo living room is furnished with upholstered *equipal* chairs and couch.

BELOW: This two-story bungalow has a secluded roof terrace.

OPPOSITE: Twisting mahogany tree trunks support the Palapa Beach Club's thatched roof.

❊ HACIENDA SAN GABRIEL DE LAS PALMAS

Amacuzac, Morelos

DATING BACK TO 1529, Hacienda San Gabriel de las Palmas was the fifth Franciscan monastery built by the Spanish crusaders in the New World. Located forty minutes south of Cuernavaca, the ancient sanctuary has thick stone walls and colossal-size rooms with barrel-vaulted ceilings. Rooms lead into rooms that pass into cloistered courtyards and candlelit terraces. Dramatic botanical gardens filled with birds and butterflies dot the sixty-two-acre estate. ❊ In 1558, the missionaries abandoned the monastery and San Gabriel was converted into a sugar plantation. Eventually it became Mexico's top-producing sugar mill in 1914. During the Mexican Revolution, the estate briefly served as headquarters for rebel leader Emiliano Zapata. ❊ The hacienda's contemporary phase began in 1970 when Jorge Fenton acquired the property and began filling it in the grand style of the plantation owners with Colonial antiques and artifacts. In 1991, he passed the property on to his son, Juan, who spent the next three years working with partner Alejandro de la Peña Razo on a painstaking and earnest renovation effort before opening the estate to the public as an inn. Poignantly aware of the historic nature of their project, they feel that they are contributing a chapter to the history of San Gabriel de las Palmas. In addition to their work in preserving the estate, they hope to be remembered for their cultural studies programs, which include a weeklong course about native medicinal plants and another about the folk traditions of the Day of the Dead. ❊

OPPOSITE: Sculpted topiary provides entry to the reflecting pool.
ABOVE: Sturdy dark-wood antiques comprise most of the furniture. Fenton-family heirlooms line the walls.

ABOVE: Flowering vines cover the massive stone walls of the old hacienda.

RIGHT: The long, narrow reflecting pool has four fonts that spout bowl-shaped shimmers of water.

OPPOSITE: A huge one-hundred-twenty-year-old *amate* tree shelters every table on the dining patio. True to its name, the hacienda is home to some fifteen varieties of palm.

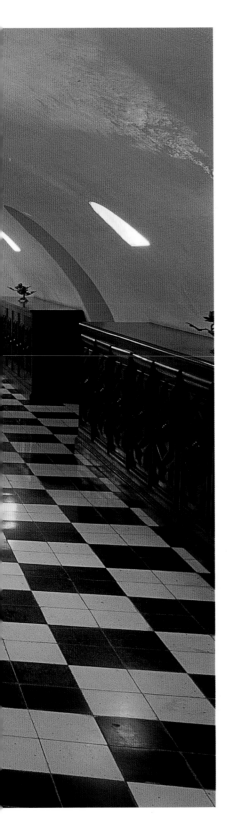

LEFT: When seated at the regal oak dining table with the checkerboard floor underfoot, you feel like a figure in a romantic chess game.

BELOW: The old Spanish-style kitchen is covered with brown and cream Puebla tiles. Its horseshoe-shaped counter holds nine burners, which allow several chefs to work simultaneously.

OPPOSITE: Designed by Jorge Fenton in 1980, it took a local carpenter a full year to carve the intricate four-poster bed located in the El Coronel Room.

ABOVE: The El Capitán Room has a seafaring theme with its paintings of sailing ships and one of a grizzly captain.

✲ LA CASA QUE CANTA

Zihuatanejo, Guerrero

LA CASA QUE CANTA MEANS "the house that sings." Bougainvillea abounds and the thatched-roof hotel appears to tumble down the cliffs into the Zihuatanejo Bay. "The structure is more like sculpture really than architecture," says Enrique Muller, the *maestro* responsible for its lyrical 1993 design. "I had to create a style that would work on such steep slopes to figure a way to integrate them into the construction." ✻ French-born owner Jacques Baldassari sought to create a hotel that was intimate, sophisticated, and shamelessly romantic. The twenty-four guest rooms are named after popular Mexican songs, such as "Besame Mucho" ("Kiss Me a Lot"), "Rayito de Luna" ("Moonbeam"), and "Sabor a Mi" ("Taste of Me"). All rooms have partially shaded balconies with breathtaking views of the bay. The choicest suites have separate bedrooms and open-air living areas with secluded plunge pools. There are no bedside alarm clocks, no dissonant sounds at all—just the squawking gulls and the restful lullaby of the waves meeting the rocky shore. ✻

ABOVE AND OPPOSITE: There are two gorgeous pools here. Perched on the cliff, the freshwater "infinity" pool has a special curved edge that creates the optical illusion of water overflowing directly into the Pacific. Closer to the crashing waves is a free-form saltwater pool and connecting whirlpool.

OPPOSITE: Dusk, as seen from the dining terrace, is the sacred hour here. The sensational sunset is the best show in town.
LEFT: The complex is entirely composed of natural materials. Architect Enrique Muller explains: "We wanted to give the impression that the structure had just risen from the earth."
BELOW: The tranquil swimming pools are reserved exclusively for the use of hotel guests.

RIGHT: The lobby showcases a marvelous array of regional crafts. Among the pottery displayed are black pots from Chihuahua, ceramic animals from Oaxaca, and a green pineapple jar from Michoacán. The star-shaped light fixtures are from Jalisco.

BELOW: Also in the lobby are white corn-husk flowers, punched-clay lamps from Jalisco, and a "Tree of Life" wreath from Metapec. The ceramic female figure is from Oaxaca and the varnished wicker lion table is from Michoacán. The *palapa* roof is made from palm thatch.

ABOVE AND RIGHT: Each evening, guests find their snowy-white bedspreads covered with enchanting arrangements of fresh leaves and flower petals—love birds one day, a peacock or a fanciful butterfly the next. It takes the maids twenty minutes to make each bed. Fresh petals also find their way into soap trays, toilet-tissue rolls, and washcloths.

OPPOSITE AND LEFT: In the lobby, chairs from Michoacán pay homage to artists Frida Kahlo and Diego Rivera.
BELOW: The hotel's three guest wings are named Sol, Mar, and Luna (sun, sea, and moon).

❉ EL TAMARINDO

Cihuatlan, Jalisco

EVEN WITH A MAP, El Tamarindo is a little tricky to find. A forty-minute drive from the Manzanillo airport, the resort's private road winds through dusty villages, tropical rain forest, and banana and coconut plantations. The two-thousand-acre nature reserve includes ten miles of unspoiled beaches, coves, cliffs, and reefs. It was originally the home of Mexican banker Roberto Hernández, a prominent conservationist. ❊ Designed to blend as unobtrusively as possible with its natural surroundings, the resort features simple, undulating lines, indigenous building materials, and an earthy color scheme. Water pipes and electrical cables are hidden underground. The rustic elegance is especially romantic at night, when the paths are lit by hundreds of *luminarias* (candles tucked into paper bags). ❊ Nearby is the 18-hole, 6,682-yard, par-72 golf course. Carving a golf course out of a rain forest might seem a formidable task, but it didn't faze architects Robert Trent Jones Jr. and David Fleming. "When we started in 1998 it was wild," Fleming recalls. "I was nicknamed Indiana Jones, and we had amazing adventures with the wildlife—jaguars and wild boars, sea turtles and parrots. But don't worry, the dangerous ones don't golf." ❊ The spectacular jungle-and-sea golf course was designed around environmentally protected areas. The result inspires and challenges the most jaded players. Fortunately, two waiters maintain a vigil at a bar beside the ninth hole, ever ready to succor golfers with drinks and a barbecue. ❊

OPPOSITE: The style of El Tamarindo's twenty-nine freestanding bungalows might be called "ZenMex," an innovative blending of rustic *palapa* architecture with a subdued Asian-inspired palette and sleek minimalist decor.
ABOVE: Each bungalow has its own dipping pool with a mini waterfall.

ABOVE: The dining room's *palapa* roof is held aloft by a dozen one-hundred-year-old strangler-root palm trunks. The chef buys fresh fish from the boats that pull into the resort's beach. Ceviche, giant prawns barbecued over coconut husks, and sautéed octopus with garlic, green pepper, and white wine are a few of the house specialties.

RIGHT, TOP: Open floor plans give the interiors a feeling of serenity.

RIGHT, BOTTOM: Pleasing curves and minimalist decor, such as a bowl filled with a few exquisite seashells and a pile of smooth gray stones, make for a tranquil entrance into the dining room.

OPPOSITE: In the uncluttered space, a mound of ripe grapefruits becomes a work of art.

ABOVE: The poolside lounging and dining area includes the simple adornment of a stone pile.

RIGHT: The sinuous "infinity" pool seems to disappear into the ocean.

contact information

Las Alamandas
Apartado Postal 201
San Patricio Melaque, Jalisco 48980
Tel: 3/285-5500
Fax: 3/285-5027
Email: alamanda@zonavirtual.com.mx

Casa de Espíritus Alegres
La Ex-Hacienda la Trinidad No. 1
Marfil, Guanajuato 36250
Tel/Fax: 4/733-1013
Email: casaspirit@aol.com

La Casa de la Marquesa
Madero No. 41
Querétaro, Querétaro 76000
Tel: 4/212-0092
Fax: 4/212-0098
Email: resven@albec.net.mx

Casa de Sierra Nevada
Hospicio No. 35
San Miguel de Allende, Guanajuato 37700
Tel: 4/152-7040
Fax: 4/152-1436
Email: sierranevada@mpsnet.com.mx

Casa Luna
Playa la Ropa
Zihuatanejo, Guerrero 40880
Tel: 7/554-2743
Fax: 7/554-4792
Email: ciprian@aol.com

Casa Luna B&B
Pila Seca No. 11
San Miguel de Allende, Guanajuato 37700
Tel/Fax: 4/152-1117
Email: casaluna@unisono.net.mx

La Casa Que Canta
Camino Escenico a Playa la Ropa
Zihuatanejo, Guerrero 40880
Tel: 7/554-6529
Fax: 7/554-7900
USA & Canada: 1-888-523-5050
Email: casaquecanta@podernet.com.mx

Casas de Careyes
Km. 53 Carr. Barra de Navidad–Puerto Vallarta
Costa Careyes, Jalisco 48980
Tel: 3/351-0240
Fax: 3/351-0246
Email: careyesg@prodigy.net.mx

Casa Vieja
Eugenio Sue No. 45, Col. Polanco
Mexico City, D.F. C.P. 11560
Tel: 5/282-0067
Fax: 5/281-3780
Email: cvieja@mail.internet.com.mx

Hacienda de Cortés
Apartado Postal 430
Cuernavaca, Morelos 62000
Tel: 7/315-8844
Fax: 7/315-0035
Email: informacion@haciendadecortes.com

Hacienda Katanchel
Tixkokob, Yucatán 97470
Tel: 9/923-4020
Fax: 9/923-4000
USA & Canada: 1-888-882-9470
Email: hacienda@mail.mda.com.mx

Hacienda San Gabriel de las Palmas
Km. 114 Carr. Federal Mexico-Acapulco
Amacuzac, Morelos 62640
Tel: 7/348-0636
Fax: 7/348-0113
Email: sgabriel@starnet.net.mx

Hotel Camino Real Oaxaca
Cinco de Mayo No. 300
Oaxaca, Oaxaca 68000
Tel: 9/516-0611
Fax: 9/516-0732
Email: oax@caminoreal.com

Hotel Casa del Balam
Apartado Postal 988
Mérida, Yucatán 97000
Tel: 9/924-2150
Fax: 9/924-5011
Email: balamhtl@finred.com.mx

Hotel Hacienda Chichén
Apartado Postal 988
Mérida, Yucatán 97000
Tel: 9/924-2150
Fax: 9/924-5011
USA & Canada: 1-800-624-8451
Email: balamhtl@finred.com.mx

Hotel Posada Coatepec
Hidalgo No. 9, esq. Aldama
Coatepec, Veracruz 91500
Tel: 2/816-0544
Fax: 2/816-0040
Email: posada@edg.net.mx

Las Mañanitas
Apartado Postal 1202
Cuernavaca, Morelos 62000
Tel: 7/314-1466
Fax: 7/318-3672
Email: mananita@intersur.com

Mesón Sacristía de la Compañía
6 Sur No. 304, Callejón de los Sapos
Puebla, Puebla 72000
Tel: 2/242-3554
Fax: 2/232-4513
Email: sacristia@mail.g-networks.net

Posada del Tepozteco
Paraíso No. 3
Barrio de San Miguel
Tepoztlán, Morelos 62520
Tel: 7/395-0010
Fax: 7/395-0323
Email: tepozhot@prodigy.net.mx

El Tamarindo
Apartado Postal 24
Cihuatlan, Jalisco 48970
Tel: 3/351-5032
Fax: 3/351-5070
Email: tamarindo@ghmmexico.com

Villa Montaña
Patzimba No. 201, Col. Vista Bella
Morelia, Michoacán 58090
Tel: 4/314-0231
Fax: 4/315-1423
Email: hotel@villamontana.com.mx

acknowledgments

We wish to express our gratitude to Sectur and to Mexicana Airlines, without whose generous support this book would not have been possible. Jorge Gamboa and Cecilia Morfin of the Mexican Tourist Office in Los Angeles, Lourdes Audiffred of Sectur, and Nick Karahalios and Hector Alvarez of Edleman Public Relations were each instrumental and ever so helpful in coordinating the logistics of our travels. We thank them profusely. ✵ Needless to say, we are grateful to all of the hotel owners and managers for their marvelous creativity, helpfulness, and generosity, which made our work such a delight: Isabel Barbachano-Gordon at Hotel Hacienda Chichén and Hotel Casa del Balam, Mónica Hernández and Aníbal González at Hacienda Katanchel, Justo Fernandez III at Hotel Posada Coatepec, Leobardo Espinosa at Mesón Sacristía de la Compañía, Ruben Cerda at Las Mañanitas, Alejandro Camerena at Posada del Tepozteco, Peter Maxwell at Hotel Camino Real Oaxaca, Carol and the late Joan Summers and Betsy McNair (our fairy godmother) at Casa de Espíritus Alegres, Dianne Kushner at Casa Luna B&B, James Sprowls at Casa de Sierra Nevada, Juan Pablo Urquiza and Carmelita González de Cosío de Urquiza at La Casa de la Marquesa, Luis Sosa at Casa Vieja, Juan Fenton and Alejandro de la Peña Razo at Hacienda San Gabriel de las Palmas, Patsy and Joe LoGiudice at Casa Luna, Ivonne and Jacques Baldassari and the delightful staff at La Casa Que Canta, Gian Franco Brignone and Giorgio Brignone at Casas de Careyes, Isabel Goldsmith and Ernesto Ponce de León at Las Alamandas, Ji Hyun Park at El Tamarindo, Eva and Philippe de Reiset at Villa Montaña, and Dr. Mario González Ulloa of Hacienda de Cortés. ✵ We thank John Wilcock for all of his hard work gathering material and writing the first stages of the text. ✵ We offer eternal gratitude to our true-blue, kind, and wise agents, Sarah Jane Freyman and Amy Rennert. And for their personal support on this project, *abrazos* to Hugh Levick, Dave Barrett, Leigh Hyams, Nancy Gallagher Shapiro, Nancy Steiny, and Susan McKinney de Ortega. ✵ Lastly, we thank Chronicle Books editors Nion McEvoy, Leslie Jonath, and Jodi Davis; copy editor Mark Nigara; and designer Vivien Sung. They are just the greatest.

— M.L. AND G.H.